SCREAMS OF SILENCE

RESHMI HAQUE

Contents

ONE

You were the sunshine
to my gloomy days
You were the
moonlight to my
darker nights
You were
everything a heart
could ever desire

TWO

I wished you to stay.
But you left without a say.
As if you found out a
way.
Leaving my heart cold as
the clay.

No more I want to pray.
Nor any feelings left to
display.
But I'll make a promise
today.
Won't allow you ever to
betray.

THREE

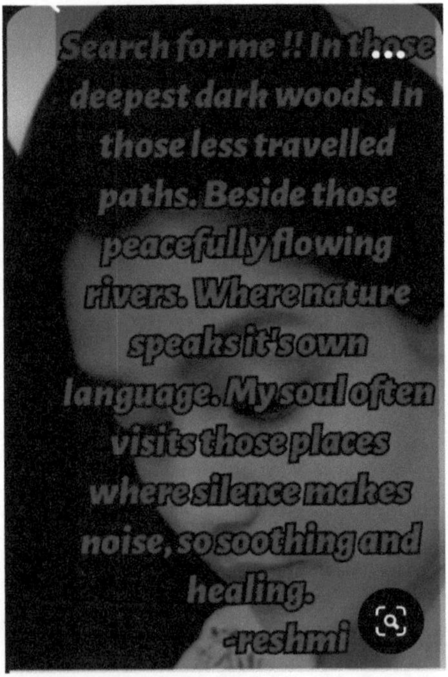

Search for me !! In those
deepest dark woods. In
those less travelled
paths. Beside those
peacefully flowing
rivers. Where nature
speaks it's own
language. My soul often
visits those places
where silence makes
noise, so soothing and
healing.
-reshmi

FOUR

A soul that danced to the hearbeat,
A soul that longed for that eternal peace.
Deepest are the wounds now,
and so are the scars.
A soul that needs to heal,
for it seems as if a huge deal.
Hope someday, it would dance to the beats again,
Hope someday, it would find that eternal peace again.

~Reshmi Haque~

FIVE

CONFLICT

Constant conflict between heart and mind.
Serenity of soul, which I lack to find.
Heart says hold on for a while,
whereas mind says move on with a smile.
What should I do, it leads to confusion.
Strenuous to figure out, this strange illusion.
Dicision was mine, to drift apart.
So why do I dwell, with a strangely aching heart.
A dilemma that's driving me insane.
Will you call me out once, and I'll try to explain.

~Reshmi~

SIX

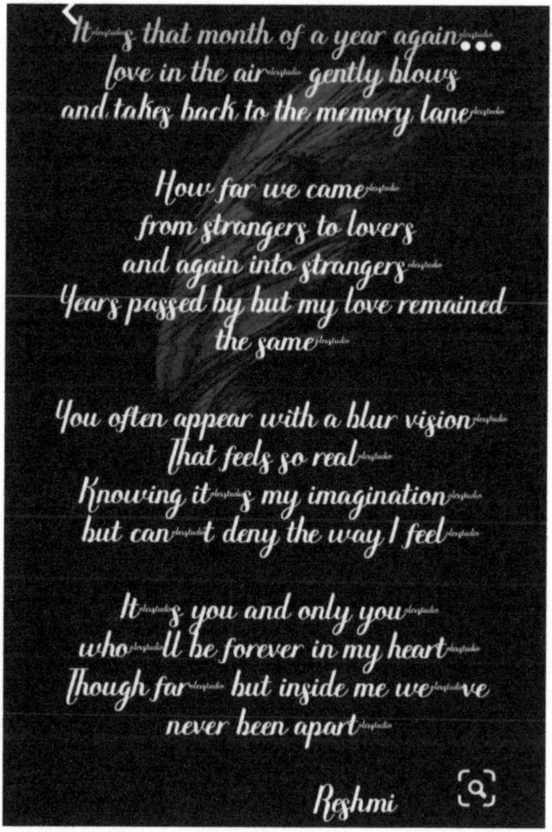

It's that month of a year again...
love in the air gently blows
and takes back to the memory lane

How far we came
from strangers to lovers
and again into strangers
Years passed by but my love remained
the same

You often appear with a blur vision
That feels so real
Knowing it's my imagination
but can't deny the way I feel

It's you and only you
who'll be forever in my heart
Though far but inside me we've
never been apart

Reshmi

SEVEN

A sweet smell floats in the air,
with every gentle breeze.
That tenderly caresses,
and disapears among the trees.
Why do I feel your presence,
when you are miles apart.
With faded memories I live
and a broken heart.
Or you too feel that void.
Tell me, do I ever cross your mind?
Thoughts which you can't avoid.
And that love, from where would you find?

Reshmi

EIGHT

Those pleasant days....
All I remember is, those
pleasant old days.
When you were around, as
warm sunlit rays.
How can I deny, that
constant pull towards you.
Unexplainable emotions
which I went through.
But it happened, unexpected
though.
The wind of love, from where
did it blow?
Everything changed, when
our eyes did meet.
All seemed so wonderful, fair
and sweet.
Drowning in your love, was
some kind of magic.
Fully unaware of the fact,
that the end would be
tragic.....

Reshmi

NINE

So many feelings left
unshared.
So many words left
unsaid.
I should have.
I should have said, the
way I felt.
That, with every glance of
yours,
how my heart did melt.
But it's late now.
Too late to call you back.
So, I do talk to you in my
dreams now.
The courage which, in
reality I lack.
Do you, in any way feel ?
Feel my presence.

TEN

In the midst of storm, I
see in you the calmness.
Be that gentle breeze of
comfort.
Turbulent tides, kept us
from sailing, on the
ocean of love.
Leaving behind the
animosity, let us rise
above.
In the midst of chaos, I
find in you the harmony.
Be that cooling rainfall,
and let me soak in.
Internal turmoil, that
created a ghastly fire
within.
Hope, the ego dies, and
may the love win.
-Resh

ELEVEN

Once in a lifetime, you'll find someone,
who'll turn your world upside down.
Once in a lifetime, you'll feel the love,
that no one else could ever give.
Once in a lifetime, you'll meet
someone,
for whom you can climb mountains and
swim across oceans.
Once in a lifetime, you'll feel the urge,
to break all the rules and cross all
boundaries.
Once in a lifetime, you'll forget about
your self-respect and values for them.
Once in a lifetime, you'll experience the
worst phase of breaking down.
Once in a lifetime, you'll feel the burn
inside and doubt your existence.
Once in a lifetime, you'll experience,
death and rebirth process.
I may sound insane, but believe me
it'll change you.
Most definetly the whole process w
either make you or break you.

TWELVE

O dear, I still love you,
and I'll always do.
Though, destiny has played it's role,
to which we had barely any control.

Still, I have a smile on my face,
as I hold myself, with dignity and grace.
Sweet moments, which we did share,
Are the only treasure, I can swear.

So, my love, promise me !
that we will meet again.
Letting go of loneliness and pain.
Somewhere, above the rainbow of
dreams,
Or just sit beside the calmly flowing
streams.

~Reshmi Haque~

THIRTEEN

Here I stand with cold feet,
This winter night is piercing through,
So frozen and chill,
Like no life left as I stand still.

Is there any hope left,
to feel the warmth once more.
Hope the morning sun fondles
my lifeless soul.

Once just once,
sit next to me,
so that I can feel
the blood running through
the veins again.
And
Let the soul renew with zeal.

~Reshmi Haque~

FOURTEEN

A whirlwind of emotions,
buried so deep....

Surfaces every night,
and ruins her sleep....

Darker are the nights,
like never before...

Creates a chaos which hits to the core...
Still she stands tall beside the shore...
whereas her soul whispers, can't take it anymore.
Brave is she with broken heart,
Smiling all through, till her soul departs.

FIFTEEN

Sometimes you have no choice left, but to let go.
Sometimes you have to move fast, to avoid getting slow.
Sometimes you even have to live in fantasy, inorder to survive.
Yes, reality is harsh at times, it'll continue to be till we're alive.
Too many mixed feelings, too many voices.
That's what makes us human, time to make some better choices.
New days arriving it's already at our door step.
So cheers, smile and let's take anew step.

SIXTEEN

A note to self.

Keep your self away from
negativity.
Which can surely can destroy your
inner peace.
Keep distance from those who
can't value your worth.
You are strong, you can sore high.
Believe in yourself is what you
need in your life.
Spread your wings, fly high.
Do what you need to do.
There will be days, when you will
doubt yourself.
Calm down and look behind just to
see how far you came.
Why to cry over your expectations
when you are all capable to build
an empire for yourself.
Always remember you are strong
yet lovable and gentle.

SEVENTEEN

May be this is the end.
May be that's what I
should comprehand.
Distance between both,
may be the factor.
Or may be, we intended
to end the chapter.
Whatever may be the
cause, now it's over.
For which the heart
denies it's closure.
A flame that burns
within, burns with a
desire.
How do I convince the
soul, that's on wildest of
fire.
Now that we are oceans
apart.
Separation that's
piercing through my
heart.
Still I wish the best
comes your way.
In the arms of love,
forever you stay.
-Reshmi

EIGHTEEN

You ask me to fly high, but my wings are torn.
You ask me to sail upon the sea, when there is thunderstorm.
How can I climb up the mountain so high,
when I have got my limbs tied.
How can I swim across the ocean so vast, when there are raising violent tides.

Tell me now, how am I supposed to smile,
when I am left only with bruises and scars.
You ask me to dance with joy, when I am lamenting over those unreachable stars.
Instead, do me a favor, bring back the moment from the bygone days, where I can
witness once again, those bright morning rays.

NINETEEN

Here I stand, with death cold feet.
All frozen and chill.
Agonizing over some long lost dreams.
Dreams, that remained unfulfilled.

A flame, that burnt so bright,
glowing and shining with all its might.
I was ready to give all it takes.
Was ready to cross the icy frozen lakes.

But, little did I know, being at a
crossroads.
The road ahead parted it's ways.
Seemed no less than a meserable soul,
Leaving my tender heart ablaze.

Now, there's nothing left except a
shattered dream,
with a pain of loss that's so extreme,
as I am left here with an unfulfilled
dream.

~Reshmi haque~

TWENTY

Dear self, can you just give me sometime to relax.
Circumstances that has left me perplexed.

Don't rush me through the battles left unfought,
Give me some time to assemble my thoughts.

Surely, I'll rise and fight again,
All you got to do is, wait, and I'll tell you when.

Worry not ! you know me I'll never quit.
Though, my mind is getting pretty tired of it.

But for now, give me sometime to relax.
Circumstances that has left me perplexed.....

~Reshmi Haque~

9 798886 847277

Printed by Libri Plureos GmbH in Hamburg, Germany